THE Big Picture Bible Time Line

Compiled by Carol Eide

Illustrated by Chizuko Yasuda
Designed by Carolyn Gillmon

Gospel Light

ISBN 0-8307-1472-3

Scriptures used in this book are from:
NIV: The *Holy Bible, New International Version.* Copyright 1973, 1978, 1984 International Bible Society. Used by permission of Zondervan Bible Publishers.

How to make clean copies from this book

You may make copies of this book with a clean conscience if:

- you (or someone in your organization) are the original purchaser;
- you are using the copies you make for a noncommercial purpose
  (such as teaching or promoting a ministry) within your church or organization;
- you follow the instructions provided in this book.

However, it is illegal for you to make copies if:

- you are using the material to promote, advertise or sell a product or service
  other than for ministry fund-raising;
- you are using the material in or on a product for sale;
- you or your organization are not the original purchaser of this book.

By following these guidelines you help us keep our products affordable. Thank you.
Gospel Light

Contents

The time line in this book illustrates major Bible events and presents them in chronological order. The dating of events generally follows the dates suggested by the *New International Version Study Bible*.

Old Testament Time Line

PART 2: HISTORY

PART 3: POETRY

PART 4: MAJOR PROPHETS

PART 5: MINOR PROPHETS

New Testament Time Line

Help Your Students Take Time into Their Own Hands—

20 Bible Time Line Ideas for Children, Youth and Adults

This Bible Time Line can be used in a multitude of ways with people of all ages. Any Bible story or portion of Scripture can be brought to life and better understood in the context of history. A time line will bring home the fact that the Bible tells about real people facing real-life challenges—and that throughout history God has been actively involved in people's lives!

Here are some suggestions for using this Bible Time Line:

CHILDREN (GRADES 1-6)

- **EARLY ARRIVALS:** Make copies of consecutive sections of the time line. A child who arrives early to Sunday School or another children's program can color the pictures. Mount the colored sections on a wall to build a time line in your classroom.

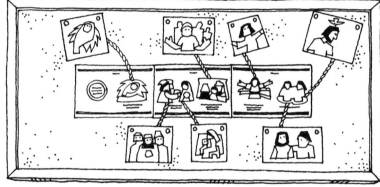

- **BULLETIN BOARDS:** Copy three or four sections of the time line. Attach them to a bulletin board. From *Bible Pictures for Children, Sets 1-4* (see "Bible Teaching Resources" on p. 73) or your church's picture file, find one or two pictures which illustrate each section of the time line. String yarn between time line sections and the appropriate pictures (see sketch).

- **ATTENDANCE BUILDER:** Make a copy of one time line section for each child in your class. Early in the week mail a section to each child. Invite the child to color the section and bring it with him or her to Sunday School or other children's program the following week. Include a comment such as, "Without you our Bible Time Line won't be complete!"

- **BIBLE LEARNING ACTIVITY:** Provide copies of time line sections for children. Before coloring his or her section, each child locates and reads the appropriate Bible reference. Children work together to display colored time line sections.

■ **FAMILY ACTIVITY KIT:** Provide copies of time line sections for children to take home to their families. Include a note which encourages family members to work together coloring and displaying time line.

■ **MUSICAL PASS-ALONG GAME:** Place copies of time line sections facedown in the center of a circle of chairs. Children sit in chairs and pass around a beanbag as music is played on a cassette player. When the music stops, child holding the beanbag chooses a time line section and briefly tells what happened in that Bible story. Continue game until each player has had a turn or until all time line sections have been chosen.

■ **JOURNAL:** Photocopy a set of time line sections for each child. Staple each set together in booklet form, using construction paper for front and back covers. Children locate and read Bible references, then use crayons or felt pens to color time line pictures. Children record what they learned from the Bible passage by writing a short paragraph at the top of the picture.

■ **TIME LINE MIX-UP:** Copy a set of time line sections for two or more teams of four or five players each. Mix up the order of each set of time line sections. Teams compete to place sections in correct order. *Variation:* Place copies of 10-20 time line sections on floor. While two or three children cover their eyes, mix the order of five or six sections. Children uncover eyes and try to place time line sections in the correct order.

■ **MAP STUDY:** Provide a copy of *Bible Maps for Children* (see "Bible Teaching Resources" on p. 73) or a Bible atlas. Child reads Scripture reference on a time line section to discover location of the event or person pictured on the time line. Child finds location on map and letters name of location on large index card. Tape card below the time line section.

- **CONCENTRATION GAME:** Place copies of two sets of time line sections facedown on the floor. Children take turns turning over two sections at a time, trying to find two matching sections. Continue playing until all sections have been matched.

- **TIME LINE CLUES:** When ten or more time line sections are displayed in your classroom, play a guessing game with children. Give three clues for a selected section. Children try to identify the section. Examples of clues might be, "I'm thinking of an event that was sad." "I'm thinking of a brave action of a Bible hero." "I'm thinking of a time God's people obeyed God."

- **PICTURE MATCH:** Place copies of five or six time line sections on table-top or floor. Also provide a Bible picture which illustrates each section (see "Bible Teaching Resources," p. 73). Children try to match each picture with the correct time line section.

- **MISSING PICTURES:** Photocopy time line sections with a strip of paper placed over the illustrations. Give each child a section. Child finds and reads the Scripture reference and then draws a picture in the blank space.

YOUTH/ADULT

- **YOU ARE HERE:** Make a copy of each section of the time line, connect the sections in order and post the completed line in your Sunday School or Bible study classroom. Place the "You are here" arrow (see "Clip Art," p. 69) on the time line to show the portion of history represented in the Bible passage you are studying.

- **OVERHEAD TRANSPARENCIES:** Make transparencies of individual time line sections. Show sections on overhead projector to introduce and/or illustrate Bible studies.

- **ATTENDANCE MOTIVATOR:** Make a copy of one time line section for each participant in your Bible study group. Five or six days before your group meets mail a section to each person. Invite him or her to bring section to Bible study the following week. Include a comment such as "Without you our Bible Time Line won't be complete!"

- **STUDY RECORD:** As a group, plot your Bible coverage by marking on a completed time line those events that you have studied. Set goals to cover specific sections of biblical history and track your progress using one or more of the shapes provided in this book (see "Clip Art," p. 71). Celebrate when you reach your goals!

- **SERMON/BIBLE STUDY ILLUSTRATIONS:** Make copies of one or more time line sections as a teaching aid for sermons or Bible studies. Distribute sections to participants encouraging them to take notes on the reverse side of each section.

- **INDIVIDUAL TIME LINES:** Photocopy time line sections, reducing them in size. Provide these copies to participants in Bible study groups. Suggest participants make their own time lines as aids to Bible study.

- **ATTENTION GETTER:** Place copies of ten or more time line sections on table. As group participants enter, ask them to work together to place the sections in chronological order.

How to Make a Bible Time Line

Follow these easy steps:

1. Photocopy each section of the time line (there are 68 sections) and the "You are here" arrow (see Clip Art on page 69).

2. Place pages in order next to each other and match heavy lines. Tape the pages together on the back-side of time line.

3. Mount time line and arrow on wall using thumb-tacks or masking tape loops. (The completed time line measures approximately 62 feet. You may need to make several rows, spiral the time line around the room or display only a portion at a time.)

Optional:

- Color the time line sections and the arrow.

- Before taping sections together, mount each page on a colored background (so a strip of color shows along each long edge of the page).

- Laminate each section for durability and for reuse with water base transparency markers.

- You may want to enlarge each section of the time line if you have access to a photocopier with that capability.

Tools and Supplies:

- Photocopy machine and paper
- Transparent tape
- Thumbtacks or masking tape

Optional:

- Felt markers
- Rubber cement or glue sticks
- Scissors
- Construction paper in a variety of colors
- Typewriter and paper (to add to or customize the time line)

In the beginning God created the heavens and earth.

Creation

Genesis 1:1—2:25

Adam and Eve—The Fall

Genesis 3:1-24

Noah's Ark

Genesis 6:1-22

The Flood

Genesis 7:1—9:17

The Tower of Babel
Genesis 11:1-9

Abraham Obeys God
Genesis 12:1-9

Isaac Is Born
Genesis 15:1-6; 21:1-7

Isaac and Rebekah
Genesis 24:1-67

Jacob's Dream
Genesis 28:10-22

Joseph Is Sold into Slavery
Genesis 37:1-36

Joseph Explains Pharaoh's Dream

Genesis 41:1-40

Joseph's Brothers Come to Egypt to Buy Food

Genesis 42:1—45:28

Sometime Between 1000 and 2000 B.C.

Job Afflicted
Job 1:1—2:10

Job Restored
Job 42:7-17

Joseph's Family Moves to Goshen
Genesis 46:1-7, 26-34; 47:1-12

Joseph Dies
Genesis 50:22-26

Israel Enslaved in Egypt
Exodus 1:1-22

Baby Moses
Exodus 2:1-10

The Burning Bush
Exodus 3:1—4:17

Moses Confronts Pharaoh
Exodus 5:1—6:1

The Plagues
Exodus 7:8 —11:10

The Red Sea Crossing
Exodus 13:17—14:31

The Ten Commandments
Exodus 19:14—24:18;
Deuteronomy 5:1-33

Israel Disobeys God
Exodus 32:1-35;
Deuteronomy 9:7-29

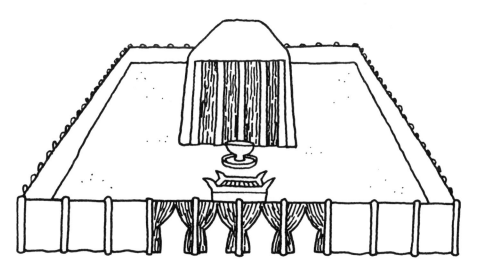

The Tabernacle
Exodus 36:8-38

The Ark of the Covenant
Exodus 37:1-9

**God Leads the Israelites
in the Desert**
Numbers 9:15-23

Joshua and Caleb
Numbers 13:1—14:45

Rahab

Joshua 2:1-24

Crossing the Jordan

Joshua 3:1-17

1406 B.C.

Jericho
Joshua 6:1-27

Achan
Joshua 7:1-26

The Gibeonites
Joshua 9:1-27

Conquering Canaan
Joshua 10:1—13:7

Joshua Divides the Land
Joshua 13:8—21:45

Joshua's Last Days
Joshua 23:1—24:33

Sometime During the Era When the Judges Led Israel

Ruth and Naomi
Ruth 1:1-22

Boaz
Ruth 2:1-23

Israel Worships Idols
Judges 2:6-23

Othniel
Judges 3:7-11

Deborah

Judges 4:1—5:31

Israelites Hide from the Midianites

Judges 6:1-10

Gideon Tests God
Judges 6:11-40

The Midianites Are Defeated
Judges 7:1-25

Jephthah
Judges 11:1—12:7

Samson
Judges 13:1—16:31

Samuel Presented to Eli
1 Samuel 1:1—2:11

Samuel Leads Israel
1 Samuel 3:1—4:1

The Philistines Capture, Then Return the Ark of the Covenant

1 Samuel 4:1-11; 5:1—7:1

Saul, Israel's First King

1 Samuel 8:1—10:27

Samuel Anoints David
1 Samuel 16:1-13

Goliath
1 Samuel 17:1-58

David and Jonathan
1 Samuel 20:1-42

David Spares Saul's Life
1 Samuel 24:1-22

1010 B.C.

Saul's Death
1 Samuel 31:1-13;
1 Chronicles 10:1-12

David Becomes King
2 Samuel 5:1-5;
1 Chronicles 11:1-3

The Ark of the Covenant Is Brought to Jerusalem
2 Samuel 6:1-15;
1 Chronicles 13:1-14

Nathan the Prophet
2 Samuel 7:1-29;
1 Chronicles 17:1-15

Mephibosheth
2 Samuel 9:1-13

Bathsheba
2 Samuel 11:1—12:25

David Flees Absalom
2 Samuel 15:1-36

David Returns as King
2 Samuel 19:8-43

David Builds an Altar to God

2 Samuel 24:18-25;
1 Chronicles 21:18-26

Solomon Becomes King

1 Kings 1:28-53;
1 Chronicles 29:21-25

The Temple Is Built
1 Kings 5:1—6:38; 7:13-51;
2 Chronicles 2:1—4:22

The Queen of Sheba
1 Kings 10:1-13;
2 Chronicles 9:1-12

930 B.C.

During This Era:
King of Israel—Baasha
King of Judah—Asa

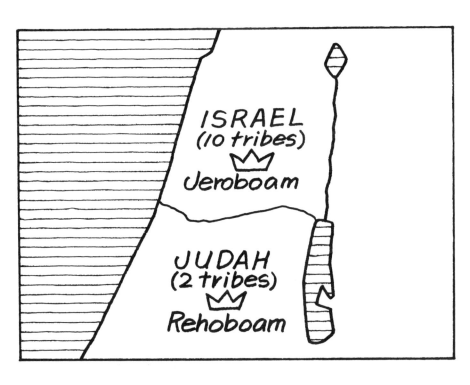

The Kingdom Is Divided
1 Kings 12:1-33;
2 Chronicles 10:1—11:17

The People Worship Idols
1 Kings 14:1-20

900 B.C.

Egypt Attacks Jerusalem
1 Kings 14:21-31;
2 Chronicles 12:1-16

King Ahab and Jezebel (I)
1 Kings 16:29-34

(I)=Israel

During This Era:
Prophet of Judah—Obadiah

Elijah and the Prophets of Baal (I)
1 Kings 18:16-46

Elijah and Elisha (I)
1 Kings 19:19-21

(I)=Israel

850 B.C.

During This Era:
King of Israel—Joram
Kings of Judah—Jehoram, Athaliah

King Ahab (I) Dies
1 Kings 22:29-40

Elijah (I) Is Taken to Heaven
2 Kings 2:1-14

(I)=Israel

800 B.C.

During This Era:
Kings of Israel—Jehoahaz, Jehoash
King of Judah—Amaziah

King Jehu (I)
2 Kings 9:1-13

King Joash (J) Repairs the Temple
2 Kings 12:1-18;
2 Chronicles 24:1-14

(I)=Israel; (J)=Judah

During This Era:
Kings of Israel—Zechariah, Shallum, Menahem, Pekahiah, Pekah, Hoshea
King of Judah—Jotham

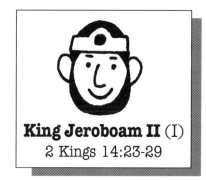

King Jeroboam II (I)
2 Kings 14:23-29

Jonah (N)
Jonah 1:1—4:11

Amos (I)
Amos 1:1—9:15

King Azariah (J)
2 Kings 15:1-7

(I)=Israel; (J)=Judah; (N)=Nineveh

King Hoshea (I)
2 Kings 17:1-6

Hosea (J)
Hosea 1:1—14:9

King Ahaz (J)
2 Kings 16:1-20;
2 Chronicles 28:1-27

The Fall of the
Northern Kingdom (I)
2 Kings 17:7-23

(J)=Judah; (I)=Israel

Isaiah (J)

Isaiah 9:1-7

King Hezekiah (J) **Destroys Places of Idol Worship**

2 Kings 18:1-8

(J)=Judah

640 B.C.

Nahum (N)
Nahum 1:1—3:19

Habakkuk (J)
Habakkuk 1:1—3:19

King Manasseh (J)
Worships Idols
2 Kings 21:1-18;
2 Chronicles 33:1-20

King Josiah (J)
Reads God's Word
2 Kings 23:1-3;
2 Chronicles 34:29-32

(N)=Nineveh; (J)=Judah

605 B.C.

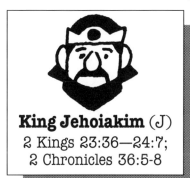

King Jehoiakim (J)
2 Kings 23:36—24:7;
2 Chronicles 36:5-8

King Zedekiah (J)
2 Kings 24:18-20;
2 Chronicles 36:11-14

600 B.C.

During This Era:
King of Judah—Jehoiachin

Daniel (B) and Others
Taken Captive
Daniel 1:1-21

Ezekiel (B) and Others
Taken Captive
Ezekiel 1:1-3

(J)=Judah; (B)=Babylon

Jeremiah (J) in Prison

Jeremiah 38:1-13

The Fall of Jerusalem (J)

2 Kings 24:20—25:26;
2 Chronicles 36:15-23

(J)=Judah

580 B.C.

The Fiery Furnace (B)
Daniel 3:1-30

Daniel (B) **in the Lion's Den**
Daniel 6:1-28

(B)=Babylon

King Cyrus (P)
2 Chronicles 36:22,23;
Ezra 1:1-11

**The First Exiles Return to
Jerusalem Under Zerubbabel**
Ezra 2:1-70;
Nehemiah 6:6—7:2

(P)=Persia

The People Worship God
in Jerusalem
Ezra 3:1-3

The Feast of Tabernacles
Ezra 3:4-6

520 B.C.

Haggai and Zechariah (J)
Ezra 5:1,2; Haggai 1:1—2:23;
Zechariah 1:1—14:21

King Darius (B)
Ezra 5:1—6:18

(B)=Babylon; (J)=Jerusalem

Queen Vashti (P)

Esther 1:1-22

Queen Esther (P)

Esther 2:1-18

(P)=Persia

Ezra Returns to Jerusalem
Ezra 7:1—8:14

Nehemiah Rebuilds Jerusalem's Walls
Nehemiah 2:11—4:23; 6:1-16

Malachi
Malachi 1:1—4:6

Ezra Reads God's Word
Nehemiah 8:1-18

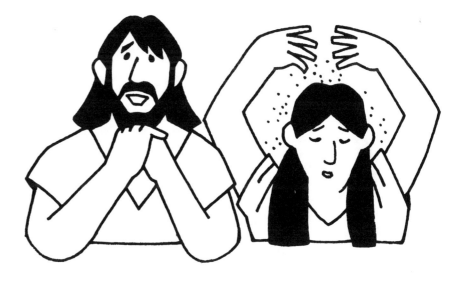

The People Ask for Forgiveness
Nehemiah 9:1-3

400 years between the Testaments

Jesus' Birth
Luke 2:1-20

The Wise Men
Matthew 2:1-12

Jesus at the Temple
Luke 2:41-52

John the Baptist Preaches
Matthew 3:1-6;
Mark 1:1-8;
Luke 3:1-20

Jesus Is Baptized
Matthew 3:13-17;
Mark 1:9-11;
Luke 3:21,22;
John 1:29-34

Jesus Is Tempted
Matthew 4:1-11;
Luke 4:1-13

Jesus Chooses Disciples
Matthew 4:18-22; 9:9-13; 10:1-4;
Mark 1:14-20; 2:13-17; 3:13-19;
Luke 5:1-11,27-31; 6:12-16;
John 1:35-51

Nicodemus

John 3:1-21

The Woman at the Well

John 4:1-42

Jesus Heals a Paralytic
Mark 2:1-12;
Luke 5:17-26

Jesus Sends Out His Disciples
Matthew 10:1-42;
Mark 6:7-13;
Luke 9:1-6

Jesus Preaches

Matthew 11—13;
Mark 4:1-34;
Luke 6:17-49; 8:1-18

Feeding the 5,000

Matthew 14:13-21;
Mark 6:30-44;
Luke 9:10-17

Jesus Walks on the Water
Matthew 14:22-33;
Mark 6:45-52;
John 6:16-21

The Transfiguration
Matthew 17:1-13;
Mark 9:2-13;
Luke 9:28-36

Lazarus
John 11:1-44

The Triumphal Entry
Matthew 21:1-11;
Mark 11:1-11;
Luke 19:28-44

Jesus Clears the Temple
Matthew 21:12-17;
Mark 11:12-19;
Luke 19:45-48
(Also see John 2:12-22)

The Last Supper
Matthew 26:17-30
Mark 14:12-26;
Luke 22:7-38;
John 13:1-30

Judas and Jesus in Gethsemane
Matthew 26:36-56;
Mark 14:32-52;
Luke 22:39-53;
John 18:1-11

The Crucifixion
Matthew 27:27-56;
Mark 15:16-41;
Luke 23:26-49;
John 19:16-37

The Resurrection
Matthew 27:57—28:15;
Mark 15:42—16:8;
Luke 23:50—24:12;
John 19:38—20:18

Jesus Appears to the Disciples
Matthew 28:16-20;
Mark 16:9-20;
Luke 24:13-48;
John 20:19—21:25

The Ascension
Luke 24:50-53;
Acts 1:1-11

Pentecost
Acts 2:1-13

Stephen Is Stoned and the Apostles Are Persecuted
Acts 5:17-42; 6:8—8:1

Saul (Paul) Meets Jesus
Acts 9:1-31

Paul Escapes
Acts 9:19-25

Peter's Vision
Acts 10:1-48

An Angel Frees Peter
Acts 12:1-19

Paul's First Missionary Journey
Acts 13:1—14:28

Paul's Second Missionary Journey

Acts 15:36—18:22

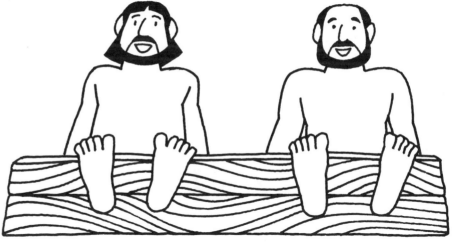

Paul and Silas in Prison

Acts 16:16-40

Priscilla and Aquila
Acts 18:18-28

Paul's Third Missionary Journey
Acts 18:23—20:38

Paul Before Festus
Acts 25:1—26:32

Paul's Shipwreck
Acts 27:1-44

Paul Writes from Prison in Rome
2 Timothy 1:1—4:22

John Exiled on Patmos
Revelation 1:1—22:21

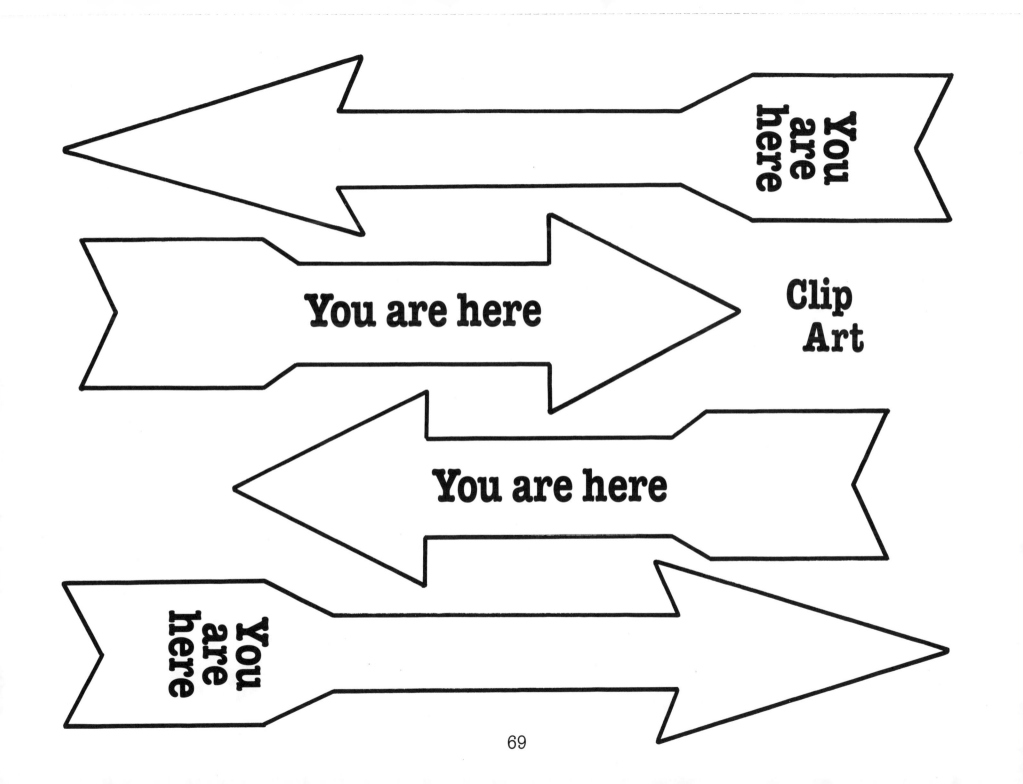

You are here

Clip
Art

You are here

You are here

69

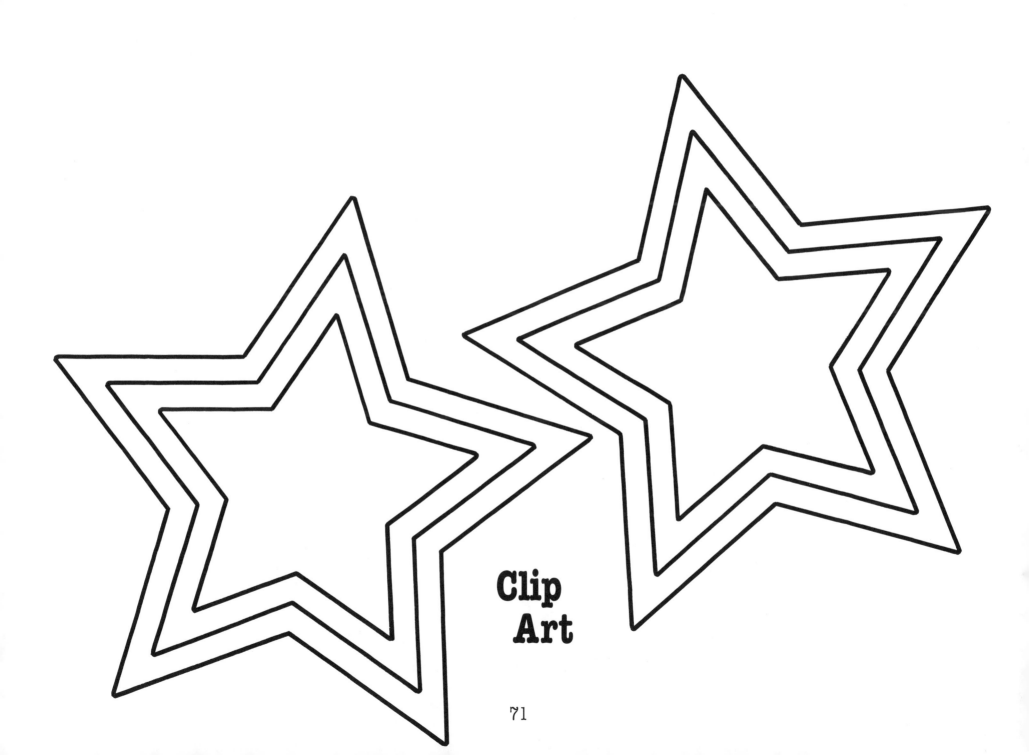

Clip
Art

71

Bible Teaching Resources/Children

Each of these teaching aids will enhance the use of the Bible Time Line. These resources are available from your Christian supplier.

What the Bible Is All About for Young Explorers is an overview of the Bible designed for children. Complete with illustrations and maps.

The Complete Bible Story Clip-Art Book is full of pictures of Bible events, characters and places. Great visuals to make your teaching materials come alive.

Bible Maps for Children help your students understand locations and boundaries of Bible lands. Includes seven Old Testament maps, three New Testament maps, plus pictures of the Tabernacle and Temple.

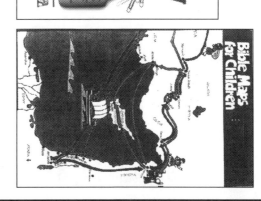

Bible Pictures for Children, Sets 1-4 provides large, full-color teaching pictures for many Bible stories. Suitable for a teaching aid during Bible story time, for bulletin board decoration, etc.

Bible Biography Series. These vividly written books help make Bible stories come alive.

Famous storyteller, Ethel Barrett, shares the excitement of a hero's life in the popular *Bible Biography Series.* These vividly written books help make Bible stories come alive.

Bible Teaching Resources/ Youth and Adult

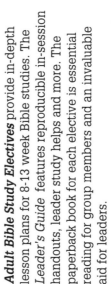

Each of these teaching aids will enhance the use of the Bible Time Line. These resources are available from your Christian supplier.

What the Bible Is All About by Dr. Henrietta Mears is a Bible study classic that takes the reader through each book of the Bible.

What the Bible Is All About, Quick Reference Edition is a basic guide to every book in the Bible, containing over 1,000 visual aids.

The Bible Visual Resource Book is a tool you can use to give your teaching more impact. Reproducible maps, charts and graphics for individual or group study. Includes the visuals from the popular *NIV Study Bible*.

Adult Bible Study Electives provide in-depth lesson plans for 8-13 week Bible studies. The *Leader's Guide* features reproducible in-session handouts, leader study helps and more. The paperback book for each elective is essential reading for group members and an invaluable aid for leaders.

Jesus of Nazareth is a unique video depicting the life of Christ from His birth through His resurrection. Use this exciting video as a small group study, Sunday School elective or as a resource for the families in your church. *Leader's Guide* and *Family Devotional* also available.

Reference Index

This index provides you with a source for information about the events shown on this Bible Time Line. To use the index, locate the title of the Bible event in the left hand column. Then turn to the appropriate pages(s) in *What the Bible Is All About for Young Explorers* (see p. 73 in this book).

BIBLE TIME LINE	*What the Bible Is All About for Young Explorers* PAGE NUMBER

BIBLE TIME LINE	PAGE NUMBER
Joshua's Last Days	62
Israel Worships Idols	66
Othniel	66, 67
Deborah	67
Israelites Hide from the Midianites	67
Gideon Tests God	67
The Midianites Are Defeated	67
Jephthah	68
Samson	68
Ruth and Naomi	72
Boaz	72
Samuel Presented to Eli	76
Samuel Leads Israel	76
The Philistines Capture, Then Return the Ark of the Covenant	76
Saul, Israel's first King	76, 77
Samuel Anoints David	78
Goliath	78
David and Jonathan	78
David Spares Saul's Life	79
Saul's Death	79, 112
David Becomes King	83, 112
The Ark of the Covenant Is Brought to Jerusalem	83, 112
Nathan the Prophet	84, 112
Mephibosheth	84
Bathsheba	85
David Flees Absalom	85
David Returns as King	85
David Builds an Altar to God	86
Solomon Becomes King	89, 113
The Temple Is Built	89, 116
The Queen of Sheba	90
The Kingdom Is Divided	90, 91, 116
The People Worship Idols	91
Egypt Attacks Jerusalem	91
King Ahab and Jezebel	92
Elijah and the Prophets of Baal	92
Elijah and Elisha	92
King Ahab Dies	93
Elijah Is Taken to Heaven	97
King Jehu	98
King Joash Repairs the Temple	99
King Jeroboam II	106
King Azariah	106
King Ahaz	106
King Hoshea	106